Die Leere Mitte

Random Access Journal

BERLIN

....
Issue n.11 ¬ 7/2021
22°C ¬ 52.4802743 ¬ 13.5441468
....

```
#include <stdio.h>
int main()
{
printf("Hello, Berlin!");
return 0;
}
```

DIE LEERE MITTE
Guidelines

Broadly accepted: Experimental and conceptual writing, theoretical papers, asemic and concrete texts, vispo, theorems, axiom collection, quantum weirdness, reviews of books addressing these topics and the like.
Texts: poetry (60 lines max. overall); prose (500-600 words max. overall). *Format*: Times New Roman 12; single line spacing; all in one .doc or .odt file. *Languages*: Catalan, Croatian, English, French, German, Italian, Russian, Spanish.
Visual: 1-3 B&W images. *Format*: jpg, tiff, png, 72-300 DPI.

Simultaneous submissions are welcome, provided that the piece is withdrawn if accepted elsewhere, as well as previously published works when properly credited. Each issue will be free to download (.pdf). A printed version will be made available through lulu.com for collectors. No reading fee; no payment or copies to contributors at present. Authors assume responsibility for the originality, intellectual property rights and ethical implications of submitted works.

submissions: leeremittemag@gmail.com
home: https://leserpent.wordpress.com/category/dlm/
twitter: @LeereMitte

Edited in Berlin by Horst Berger and Federico Federici.
ISBN 9798760716194

Cover art: Tamizh Ponni

CONTENTS

Jim Meirose
>*Yes In Those Very Same Flannel-Sleeved Snacks* p.7

John Grey
>*Anger followed by walk* p.9
>*The woman who jumped from the bridge* p.10
>*Catwalk* p.11

Howie Good
>*Gotterdammerung* p.12

Graham C. Goff
>*The Next Compartment* p.13

yours truly, the happy recluse
>*empty glass on picnic table* p.16
>*color one* p.17
>*dinner bell for god-dam eaters* p.18

Mark Young
>*House servants of German-Bohemian descent* p.19
>*From the Pound Cantos: CENTO XXVI* p.21
>*Random enthalpy or random entropy?* p.22

Mohamed Gassara
>*Claque de certitude* p.23

Paweł Markiewicz
>*a pulchritudinous sonnet* p.24

Ramsay Randall
>*for many a time* p.25
>*for Sandra* p.26
>*trompe l'oeil* p.27
>*life study* p.28

J. D. Nelson
>*at the self-help police academy* p.29
>*are you a* thimb *or a thumb?* p.30
>*royal jelly* p.31
>*david lee monkfish* p.32

Patrick Sweeney
>*senryu* p.33

On the light in, 'n sit down.

Harley, I think we should do it. It's way past time to.

Dolly, you say that each year.

Are whirlybirds? Time? Got no?

Needs to play.

Got.

Then, we do, said Harley, waving an arm. See? There's sheets there. 100 Ruled.

Space-age bullets of boxes two by them before set two of those Magnum Superior Hero snacks. Flannel-sleeved in yearly to see Chaplain Ameri-gahh.

But magnums, said Dolly—two set them before squat set coffee o' table a' table coffee a' o' a' o' a', coffee.

What?

The magnums lay coldly coffee tabled before them. Their magnums. On coldly. Lay magnums. Harley grimly replied; Do! Hop! Corkscrewer. We then, for years. Each that which says you, Dolly, are the ones. They're them. See that?

I am sorry, Harley, I really am, but; neither man nor woman nor dog ever flannel-sleeve it in yearly like that, to see Chaplain 277-316.

But, new them's to get really clearly we should, I think I do, replied Harley. Before table coffee on coldly lay magnums, theirs. See it?

No! Exactly 277-316, exactly. Buh'. Got the time?

Got?

No!

Then, lay coldly. On coffee table a' table o' coffee set squat before them u' set two magnums 'u but magnums, as, exactly! As whirlybirds are! My God, exactly, no. Dog. Play to needs. Nor woman-man, neither.

Makes sort of sense Dolly?

Hey.

Those two sat before them, by two boxes of bullets and a space-age corkscrewer. Hop! Ruled: 100 sheets. Hero's superior. So; Ameri-gahh's Chaplain see to that yearly, in their flannel-sleeved snacks. They rose a'last 'greeing completely to see that very Chaplain, yearly, in those very same flannel-sleeved snacks. Nor woman-man, neither; no issue.

Got time?

Got time?

Yes I do.

I am happy when we agree.

Me too.

Switch on the dark when leaving the room please.

Thank you.

John Grey · *Anger followed by walk*

Hot summer's day. Little girls' screaming for his attention.
He has this great need to smash their lemonade stand
all over the lawn. But he does not stay, does not bring himself down.
He listens to his lungs first. Then his hands, more accustomed
to thumping on pianos and drums. He's a musician but
this is a different kind of hot. For protection, he enlists
their youthful volition and moves on.

John Grey · *The woman who jumped from the bridge*

Something she must sleep through because, long ago,
her mother wouldn't buy her a dolly. Discovered
by a hunter with a lousy aim. Thought it was
some buck he shot. But just a young woman
in an unglamorous pose floating in the river.
The guy let go all he'd been eating.
Skin bluish-transparent. Eyes like once pristine
countries, now the subject of foreign meddling.
Inscrutable cops dragged her out.
The hunter spoke clumsily to an auditorium full of children.
"If my words don't get you I guarantee the pictures will."

John Grey · *Catwalk*

Models slink down the catwalk.
So transparent a trick.
Beating of their hearts
give them nightmares.
Scenery they pass through
is like the ogres in a children's story.
In tailoring their shapes,
they share in the illustrations.

Welcome to the Age of Autonomous Machines, where the brown bears of Kamchatka are cold, ragged, and hungry, and under perpetual ban, and rivers brim with jizz and blood, and fish have the twisted mouths of stroke victims, where saints travel incognito on New York City subways and God speaks to them in a gravelly two-packs-a-day voice, where a peeling billboard declares it's time to look ahead to the past, when the public gallows stood silhouetted at dusk against a sky of faded red plush.

Blinking like a sick mole in the harsh white light of the desert, the last of the angels steps out of his winged chariot onto the hot tarmac. Little girls in braids present him with bouquets. Jeers erupt somewhere among the hundreds of people solemnly watching the ceremonies from behind a security fence. The plainclothesmen mixing with the crowd pepper-spray everyone within range. On the tarmac, meanwhile, a military band strikes up a brassy tune that has long been a favorite of dictators around the world. Birds hum along.

I go to sleep to music, wake up to the barking of Soviet space dogs. We are apparently closer than I realized to the border of a bygone era. "Better call a repairman," I whisper to my wife, who is standing on tiptoes, peering over my shoulder. By the time the repairman arrives, it is 4 in the afternoon and the sky has a long, black crack running down the middle. As he unpacks his tools, he volunteers that he has a titanium plate in his head. I just nod. Death, when it finally comes, will have his phlegmy eyes.

Bubbles the clown was missing and Pierce had to find him before the circus train could leave. If Pierce couldn't find him on the train, it would be assumed that he had run away and the circus would be short-staffed until they found someone to fill his position.

It was late and the monkeys and their trainers reclined, smoking on their cots. The monkeys blew smoke rings and chattered amongst themselves. Occasionally, one monkey stole a pack of cigarettes from another and the trainers had to break up the fight. Pierce entered the train car during one such skirmish. He stood and watched, waiting for the uproar to subside and then asked a trainer if he had seen Bubbles. The trainer had not seen Bubbles. The trainer asked the others; they had not seen Bubbles. The trainer asked the monkeys; they had not seen Bubbles either. Pierce moved to the next train car.

The clowns were hunched over a circular table at the center of the compartment, playing cards. They passed a bottle of liquor around, but did not offer Pierce a hit. The relationship between the clowns and circus management had been contentious since they attempted to unionize a few months before.

One of the clowns was not in on the card game. He sat by the window, his chest heaving rhythmically. He had not yet removed his makeup and it was runny. Despite the smeared makeup, he identified the clown by the window as Marbles, the clown who worked with the freak show. Marbles told Pierce that Bubbles had gone into town to buy food and booze and that he should have returned a few hours before. Pierce nodded. He did not ask Marbles why he was crying. He assumed that Marbles and the bearded lady were fighting again. Pierce moved on to the next compartment.

The bearded lady sat alone in her compartment and her chest rose and fell rhythmically in front of the mirror. Her and Marbles were fighting again. When Pierce asked if she had seen the missing clown, she simply shook her head "no" and continued to shave her beard. She moaned something about how Marbles never treated her right anyhow to her reflection. Pierce moved on to the next compartment.

The lion tamers gave a collective start when Pierce entered the compartment, cowering in his presence. They winced with his every move, jumpy and on-edge. They huddled around a radio. The assistant lion tamer told Pierce that he saw Bubbles enter the train about an hour before. The lion tamers returned their focus to the radio, casting occasional nervous glances at him. Pierce moved on to the next compartment.

Bubbles slouched against the wall of the Siamese twins' compartment. He had one of the bottles of liquor open at his side. He was listening to the twins playing the piano. Pierce sat beside the clown. The twins were playing Brahms. As the song came to an end, they began to argue. The left head wanted to play Bach and the right head wanted to play Schubert. They could not reach an agreement, so the left head played Bach with her left hand and the right head played Schubert with her right head. The tunes clashed, each attempting to play over the other. Bubbles offered Pierce a hit and he accepted, closing his eyes.

yours truly, the happy recluse · *empty glass on picnic table*

Look at that empty
       glass
       100% full of air—
       & 100% full of light
            also in there.
That's two
     hundred percents at once
          simultaneously—
occupying the same space in perfect harmony.
Look at that empty
       glass
       in which space of totality—
seems so central in the glass
          but basks borderlessly.

yours truly, the happy recluse · *color one*

If GodFace has a color
it's where atoms are empty . . .
unseen/beholdingly : radiating
brainbow prisms
        liberatingly, self-recognized
where I AM is one color : *clarity*
(unstained linguistically);
self-meditative effortless deLight
        that's not lazy—
empty-atom field
        Garden E stability:
unexpelled by ego-stuck
        dust-to-dust destiny,
GodFace color *clarity*
        undammed by scenery;
beautiful or ugly mind-mirrors reflect
stainlessly : sudden-access quality
in-hearing silently...thought-free
        secret mantra 'enters'
GodSpace already.

So why say 'enter' at all?

That's [your] discovery : color one
embracing GodSky/mindcloud centrally.
Where it's *clarity* it celebrates diversity
(each one intimately) 'tween the temples
GodSpace color of
        no post or pre : deLight
dry as GodSun now
        immersing five-sense sea.

Mirror-stainlessness, feast on
reflections' clingy quality…
[this] skull-hollow bell
                rings clear
    through doomed
        down body-me,
uninterruptedly, compassionately
now/outlasting all
        failure to see;
but
waiting to die to get it
waits incurably.
Actual I AM's undyed by all
these sensory…
    necktop auras
    centerpiecing
    feast of clarity.

Mark Young · *House servants of German-Bohemian descent*

are cut off from all emotion & magic

become polymers, either in solution for coating thin films or as particles for construction

contact the manufacturer directly to receive a quote

don't participate in non-violent revolution

encourage their youth & people to attend public hospitals in France

find that silence is full of music

grapple continually with millions of animated graphics & images

have yet to provide a historical basis for their claims of an ancient origin

identify & analyze the most important trends shaping our world

join other European countries responding negatively to the ANZ Bank considering off-shoring 600 jobs

keep records written in either Czech, German, or Latin

learn sexual skills at a young age because they don't have the internet

manage the most uncompassionate, inflexible airline around

narrow down their options, pack their bags, & get ready to go operate a newly-commissioned US Navy attack submarine with an Xbox 360 controller

promote high-trust executives who fail to engender innovation by creative personnel

question the words of the mighty JIMMY

reinforce the precepts of mumbo-jumbo with the use of flash cards & black balaclavas

shoot wolves

think that integrity is the *sine qua non* of public women's shelters

undermine the foundations of democracy with unchecked party elites

validate their tickets when on trains in Italy by finding a funny looking green-blue box at the entrance of a platform & then waving their ticket on it until a green light blinks

will, under no circumstances, transfer to any other party the typefaces &/or fonts used in any *Rolling Stone* article

xray themselves regularly to ensure they're not being overrun by gallstones

yawn purely to puzzle scientists

zone out if icecream kolaches aren't included along with their coffee

Mark Young · *From the Pound Cantos: CENTO XXVI*

We were workmen in the same
village, saying nothing, super-
fluous. No love of science & letters —

the norm. Beat drums for three
days. Dragon barge, high buggy
wheels, fond of rotation, drifted

with the music. The valley is thick
with leaves, the house a shade too
solid, knocking at empty rooms

stubborn against the fact. Boredom
born out of boredom, out of nothing, a breathing in the stillness.

I sleep, I sleep not. This machinery
is very ancient; who can lift it?

Mark Young · *Random enthalpy or random entropy?*

The last contrail mounts the
stairs at midnight. Music
surrounds it; *Finlandia* by
Sibelius; which may be why
the ascent is so quiet, even
though the music does not
penetrate the contrail's
senses. The typewriter it

carries with it has passed
the becoming a burden
stage. Should have been left
behind some time back; but a
contract is a contract, & even
though Goethe has long passed,
there's still that clause in there—
passes to his heirs & successors.

Mohamed Gassara · *Claque de certitude*

Trois enfants
claquent des mains
alternativement,
circulairement.
Ils forcent les claques
en mettant dans leurs paumes
une rougeur de saumon.
Ils giflent le bonheur de l'âge,
et sur leurs lèvres,
ils accrochent une balançoire
poussant le dieu du jeu,
sans retour.
Ils sont forts, pas enfantins,
enchaînant des mains
comme pour fêter un nain circoncis.
La fumée du narguilé
sert d'encens
le grenadier querelle avec l'olivier
sur une question de longévité,
et au-dessous, les enfants songent
dans un moment à dent-meringue
lorsqu'un cri surgit
dû à une forte claque,
battant les cuisses varicelleuses du rire
et transformant les joues de poupée en briques.
Cri de victime,
on l'entoure avec des claques interminables,..
d'où naît une certitude de vie.. !

Paweł Markiewicz · *a pulchritudinous sonnet*

I am through a superb window – looking.
An angel of feeling awakes in me.
The dreamy oak-trees stand alway leafless.
The native auspicious cue is just large.

My scenery - the enchanted verdure.
The moony old barn of Ted my dear nuncle.
I am looking at a proud throng of crows.
They belong to the whiff of every times.

The springtide looks so meek-beauteous-fair,
first and foremost Morningstar - at night.
I daydream springwards window-view withal
of a dreamy Ovidian summer gale.

Homelike herbage that seems to bewitch all.
My cats want to enchant the fantasy.
Dreamed subtle morn withal notably.

gale - archaic: wind
alway - archaic: always
cue - archaic: mood
verdure - green
nuncle - archaic: uncle
throng - archaic: bevy

"But death also exists for the individual in another sense [...] it is burdened with the weight of the residues of its operations [...] the individual little by little takes on elements of stable equilibrium that charge it and prevent it from going toward new individuations [...] this heatless dust and this unenergized accumulation are the rise of passive death within the being [...]"

"Is it not true that old people, who've spent a lifetime together, start to resemble each other? Eventually they have so much in common that they not only have the same thoughts, but the same facial expressions. Why do you think that is? I hope we become so old that we share each other's thoughts... and that we get little, dry and completely identical wrinkled faces."

Ramsay Randall · *for Sandra*

I went to Jeddah, to
Manila, beaten
in the engine's time.

I stopped, went
east, then west, then
two times east,

and twice the point
that had two names
enveloped me:

it looked black but was gold.

Ramsay Randall · *trompe l'oeil*

thunderheads folded above
Iowa highway, integer
cornstalks; the clouds
flash.

the clouds burn
in themselves, light
lights hundreds on
hundreds, shading
down to primordial night.

Cardinal Guevara
poses, his episcopal
vestments - thunderhead's
pink aspect.

I am on the highway,
myself a storm
in the saddle
of the primitive function.

Ramsay Randall · *life study*

fitful night unveils
bare day. and the will,
what's left in the pan
won't start.

she leans over and
looks, solid. we left
the chains behind.
what was muscle moves.

in the black eye a
sediment of infinite
values. still awake
the sun fills the room.

J. D. Nelson · *at the self-help police academy*

the comma says
I know all of you from camp

taking pictures with a three-dollar camera
the changing of the worlds – the splice, now

away from the universe
I become the rainbow

we hear the sentences in the soup
the goosebumps kid in the commercial

eating a denim cake
a chance to see the king

um, unfounded mirror cats
morris is the champ

the planet was robbed
longhand in the garden

J. D. Nelson · *are you a* thimb *or a* thumb?

the popcorn in wednesday's sink
the color of the barn

      the blue of the growling island

the foot of the dumb door
I'm cloning a smurf's skull

the face island and alien
the wyoming hand

to be the cork of the puddle
to bee the stork of the premise

J. D. Nelson · *royal jelly*

I was a boiling shoe in the chamber of know-the-lord

        the light of the symbolism
        the shoe is here, too

I was in the king's chamber when I heard an owl

a little of the light here in broncos country

the luxury of the tongue

J. D. Nelson · *david lee monkfish*

e-e-e-e-e
    ohiowa

Patrick Sweeney · *senryu*

strip search
the worry stone
in my left front pocket

my cold deck
Mid Tang goatee
and three heart attack markers

drinking with a yamabushi
his teeth worn down
to the nub

behind torn shoji
the cat killer
is napping

the surgical precision
of chopping garlic
alone

www.ingramcontent.com/pod-product-compliance
Lightning Source LLC
Chambersburg PA
CBHW031516210526
45464CB00007B/2935